Wade Hampton III

Summer resident of North Carolina

Wade Hampton III

Summer resident of North Carolina Cashiers and Hot Springs

By

S. Robert Lathan, Jr., M.D. and Jane Gibson Nardy

Published by
Wings Publishers, LLC
P O Box 11530
Atlanta, GA 30355

Text @2014 by S. Robert Lathan, Jr., M.D. and Jane Gibson Nardy

Design and Layout by Nicola Simmonds Carmack

All rights reserved. No part of this publication may be reproduced, stored in a retrieval system, or transmitted in any form or by any means – electronic, mechanical, photocopy, recording, or any other – except for brief quotations in printed previews, without permission of the authors.

Manufactured in the United States of America

10 9 8 7 6 5 4 3 2 1
First Edition

ISBN 978-1-930897-21-2

To

The Hampton Family
Cashiers, North Carolina

Acknowledgements

The authors give special appreciation to the following persons and organizations that contributed countless hours of conversation and information sharing that gave both fullness and accuracy to this project.

Their contributions have helped to bring the importance of Wade Hampton III's life and influence on the Cashiers and Hot Springs areas to the enjoyment of many.

Will and Becky McKee – High Hampton Inn

Ann McKee Austin

Cashiers Historical Society

Jacqueline Painter of Sylva, North Carolina

Mark Jones – High Hampton Inn

Johns Hopkins Medical Center Archives

The Citadel Archives

Millie Lathan, for her insights into this project

Ginger Watkins, our Publisher

Preface

In 2006, I was the Chairman of a program presented by the Cashiers Historical Society on Wade Hampton III. In my planning, I asked Jane Nardy to speak on the geographic location of Wade Hampton's presence in Cashiers Valley. She found this research very difficult as she described as "comparing it to Elvis after death – he was seen everywhere, but no one could prove it." After considerable research for legal deeds, as well as confirmation of no written records by the South Caroliniana Library, Jane determined that Wade Hampton III's land ownership in Cashiers Valley began in 1855 and not the 1840s as suggested by previous Hampton biographies.

So how did Wade Hampton III visit the Cashiers Valley in the 1835-1855 years to achieve his renowned reputation in hunting, fishing, and outdoor activities. He did visit there with friends such as John C. Calhoun and stay for long periods with settlers including the McKinneys and Zacharys. Many of these stories have been passed through families who still are a part of Cashiers permanent residents and told in written history accounts of the area.

It is also known the Wade Hampton II had a special interest in a summer retreat in White Sulphur Springs, Virginia. There he built a Greek Revival home in 1837 called the Colonnade. Wade III and his brother Kit spent many summers enjoying the cool retreat. Wade III met his future wife, Margaret Preston during one of these summers at the Colonnade.

Another site that the Hamptons definitely visited and built a summer retreat was Warm Springs (later name changed to Hot Springs) North Carolina. The book researched and written by Jacqueline Painter in 1992 states that Wade Hampton II built a summer cottage behind the Warm Springs Hotel in the 1830s. It is ironic that Alfred Hampton, Wade Hampton III's youngest son was the person who suggested the newly rebuilt Mountain Park Hotel in Hot Springs as the site of a camp for detention of about 2000 German prisoners of war in 1919. The Hampton cottage was used for a time as the camp hospital during the "German invasion."

Wade Hampton III was truly one of the most famous and revered South Carolinians of the Nineteenth Century. But why and how did he come to the western North Carolina mountains?

This book is felt to give some clarity to the questions of when and why as well as the most important question of what made him a legend in Cashiers Valley, NC.

The marks of Wade Hampton III and his family resonate to this day in Western North Carolina in both Cashiers and Hot Springs.

Bob Lathan

Introduction

The connections between one of the most admired South Carolinians and the lush green valleys, hidden away in the mountains of Western North Carolina, of Cashiers Valley and Warm Springs began when the man was young and the land undeveloped. Wade Hampton III traveled in search of recreational activities and retreat from hot humid summers and their annoying mosquitoes of his home in South Carolina to find a paradise of game, fish and respite for his whole family. He and his descendants left a powerful and lasting mark on their found haven.

I remember well the incident... you refer to as I do many pleasant hours spent in the mountains of North Carolina.
—Quote of Wade Hampton, Sloan, 1891

Lieutenant General of the Army of Northern Virginia in 1864

Wade Hampton III

Wade Hampton I
General Wade Hampton I in 1812

Colonel Wade Hampton II
from a portrait completed in 1835
by William Scarborough

Wade Hampton III in 1840

Who was Wade Hampton?

Confederate General **Wade Hampton III** (1818-1902), later governor of South Carolina and U.S. Senator, was one of the most famous and revered South Carolinians in the Nineteenth Century. His statue, in the U.S. Capitol Statuary Hall, along with John C. Calhoun, occupies one of the two niches allotted to South Carolina.

Wade Hampton I

His grandfather, **Wade Hampton I** (1751-1835) was a trader, planter, and soldier. In the Revolutionary War he served under General Thomas Sumter and was temporarily taken prisoner by General Banestre Tarleton at Fishing Creek. He was promoted to Lt. Colonel and led a brilliant cavalry charge at Eutaw Springs. In 1786 he built the Woodlands plantation, near the new state capitol in Columbia. He was elected to Congress twice, owned plantations in South Carolina, Mississippi and Louisiana, which required the labors of over 1000 slaves. In 1809 he was promoted to General and sent to New Orleans. At that time he purchased a second cotton plantation in Mississippi and a sugar plantation in Louisiana. He was known for his love of horses, and raising and racing stallions. At the time of his death in 1835, he was considered one of the wealthiest men in America.

Wade Hampton II

His father, **Wade Hampton II** (1791-1858) lived in both a time and culture of the South when great wealth created a planter aristocracy that later experienced the ravages of the Civil War. He was a gentleman, a superb horseman and hunter, as well as a renowned agriculturist and turfman. He learned the art of politics from his father and many of the nation's leaders who were entertained at the family home, Woodlands.

At the age of twenty-two, Hampton joined the First Light Dragoons as a 2nd Lieutenant in the War of 1812. After the decisive American victory at the Battle of New Orleans, General Andrew Jackson ordered Hampton to take the victory news to President Madison in Washington, DC. Hampton famously rode one horse 750 miles in ten days to his home in Columbia, SC. From there he went on to the U.S. Capitol by boat to deliver the good news.

Wade II demonstrated his skills in land management by assisting his father in expanding the Hampton holdings in sugar plantations in Louisiana and cotton farming in Mississippi, as well as new tract of land called Millwood near the family home of Woodlands. Robert Mills, a renowned architect, designer of the Washington Monument and native South Carolinian, spent time with the Hamptons drawing a map that described the family lands in Richland County, SC.

One of his closest friends and competitors in the horseracing world was Col. Richard Singleton of the Home Place Plantation in Stateburg, SC. The Hamptons and Singleton families usually summered together at White Sulphur Springs in the mountains of Virginia. There they introduced the Greek Revival style of architecture to the Colonnade Complex. Later after renovations in the same style, Millwood became one of South Carolina's greatest mansions as well as a model, working plantation. The great lofty southern front featured six two story stone pillars in the middle with three lesser ones on each side. The grand centered steps led upwards to the mansion's wide piazza.

In 1825 while serving as aide to Governor Manning, Hampton II was promoted to Colonel of the Richland County militia and elected to the South Carolina Senate, his first and only elected office. For more than thirty years Colonel Hampton, as he was fondly called, played an important role in South Carolina politics, hosting and engaging in discussions with many dignitaries including John C. Calhoun.

When General Wade Hampton I died in 1835, the estate was divided between family members, leaving Wade Hampton II the Carolina plantations. Colonel Hampton gave more attention to the stables and bought many horses, especially from Hampton Court in England, re-establishing the Hampton stables as successful horse breeding and racing businesses. By 1840 he had become the most extensive breeder of thoroughbred horses in South Carolina. As the soil in the gulf states began to produce more cotton, Colonel Hampton was the first to diversify crops in South Carolina and experiment with new fertilizers.

Colonel Hampton died at the Walnut Ridge Plantation in Mississippi 1858 after riding his fields in the rain in his daily routine of inspecting his fields. His remains were returned to be buried in the family cemetery near Columbia. His influence had shaped the politics of South Carolina for decades. In announcing Colonel Hampton's death, the Charleston *News and Courier* described him as a

> *man of "untiring public spirit…*
> *and first gentleman of the state."*

Woodlands-Millwood complex in 1825

Conjectural drawing of Millwood House after the 1840 renovations

The Hampton family home named Millwood began as the wooded Mill Tract across the Garner's Ferry Road from Woodlands given by Wade Hampton I to Wade II as a gift on occasion of his marriage to Ann Fitzsimons in 1817. Hampton built a raised two-story cottage on the highest point surrounded by trees and necessary outbuildings. In the 30s the Hamptons engaged the services of Nathaniel Potter from Rhode Island to renovate and enlarge the home in the Greek Revival style of architecture with the six imposing tall fluted pillars with a two-story piazza running across the front.

East of Columbia near the banks of the Congaree River, Millwood and its five acres of gardens became the center of social and political life for the Hamptons and their many friends. Most of the feasts included quality meats and vegetables produced in their own fields. The massive library required two rooms and was always open to the guests.

It was a happy life. There was little of meanness or deceit or lasting sorrow to be encountered, and virtually no premonitions of tragedy, strife or insecurity for the future. Wade Hampton and his family lived in the midst of a personally owned splendor that seemed as grand and as permanent as the hills and woods and the rivers.—Wellman, 1949

At the death of Wade Hampton II in 1858, Millwood became the home and a part of the ownership of Colonel Hampton's four unmarried daughters. Millwood along with other Hampton homes of Diamond Hill and Woodlands were burned in February, 1865 at the same time that General Sherman's Union troops were marching through South Carolina with much destruction in their wake. With the guidance of Kit Hampton, the sisters rebuilt a new two-story house on another part of the property after the war.

The property consisting of the ruins left after the burning by the troops was placed on the National Register of Historic Places in 1871. Five of the iconic columns covered in vines serve as a ghostly reminder of those towering figures in South Carolina history, the three Wade Hamptons.

Millwood ruins

Wade Hampton III

*Wade Hampton III honored in Statuary Hall
in U.S. Capitol Building, Washington, DC*

Wade Hampton III Was Born To Leadership

His strength and endurance were legendary. He was a master of five plantations, growing and processing sugar in Louisiana, growing cotton in Mississippi and in his home state of South Carolina excelling in crop rotation and breeding of horses and cows. At the beginning of the Civil War, he had become one of the richest men in the South.

Wade Hampton III was born in March, 1818 in Charleston, SC, the first born of Wade II and Ann Fitzsimons Hampton. Wade Hampton was "born to the manor" and like his father, the epitome of the Southern gentleman, even surpassing him as an equestrian and sportsman. As a four year old:

His old-soldier grandfather was setting him astride a horse and clamping his baby hands around the barrel of a fowling piece.
—Wellman, 1949

He was described as one of the finest horseman in America with the ability to master any horse. When his grandfather died in 1835, his Revolutionary War sword was left to Wade III.

Wade entered the freshman class at South Carolina College at age fourteen, graduating in 1836 and continuing to read law for two more years, though he never practiced. He joined Richland County's fine cavalry company and with his six-foot stature and superb riding ability presented well at military parades.

In the summer of 1837 while vacationing with the family of Colonel Richard Singleton in White Sulphur Springs, VA, Wade III met Margaret Preston, the sister of his uncle by marriage,

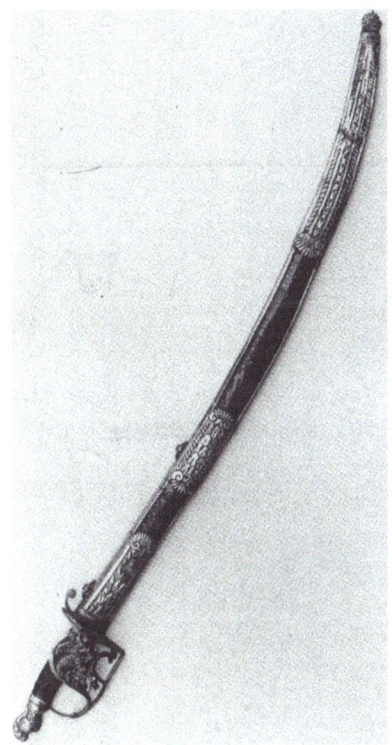

The engraved hilt of the revolutionary war sword

John Preston. A year later Wade and Margaret were married at her home in Abingdon, VA.

Margaret Preston Hampton (1818-1852) was the youngest of ten children all well educated by their parents in Abingdon, VA. She married Wade Hampton III when they were both twenty years of age and soon began their life on family property near Columbia. Five children were born to this marriage with two dying in childhood.

John Smith Preston (1809-1881) from Abingdon, VA was a lawyer, planter, politician, orator, soldier, and banker. He graduated from Hampden-Sydney College in 1825, the University of Virginia and Harvard Law in 1827. He practiced law in Virginia from 1830-1835 and Columbia, SC from 1835-1840. In 1830 he married **Caroline Martha Hampton**, daughter of General Wade Hampton I at the Hampton town home in Columbia, and returned to Abingdon to live and practice law. In 1835 he and Caroline moved from Abingdon, VA to Columbia to live with her mother in the townhouse thus beginning a life long relationship between Wade Hampton III and John Preston.

John and Caroline moved to Houmas in 1849 to manage the sugar plantations and built a large mansion facing the Mississippi River. They traveled frequently to Europe and were patrons of the famous American sculptor, Hiram Powers. After the death of Wade Hampton II, the Hampton family sold the 12,000 acre plantation for $1.5 million and the Prestons moved to South Carolina, expanding the Hampton-Preston Mansion in Columbia. Wade III was also the friend, brother-in-law, and nephew of John Preston.

Wade Hampton Takes His Place In The Family

Wade III began to travel with his father and expand their landholdings in Mississippi. From the 2500 acres of Walnut Ridge cotton and hunting plantation he amassed more than 10,000 acres with Wild Woods on the northeast shore of Lake Washington, his Mississippi house. Wade Hampton's reputation as a successful planter began to equal his prowess as a sportsman. In 1852, Margaret Preston Hampton, died at age 34 and was buried in the family cemetery in Trinity Churchyard. Wade's sisters assumed daily responsibility of the four children.

Wade III had five younger sisters, referred to affectionately as the "Aunties," who though unmarried, assumed most of the roles of nurturing and raising to adulthood the family children who suffered the loss of a parent due to war and disease.

Harriet Flud Hampton (1823-1848) Harriet died at age 25 and like the rest of the family is buried in Trinity Churchyard, Columbia.

Catherine (Kate) Pritchard Hampton (1824-1916) Kate was the surrogate mother for Kit's daughter, Annie Hampton. The last surviving sister, she was considered the family historian and graciously responded to most requests.

Ann M. Hampton (1826-1914) Ann was the surrogate mother for Sally, daughter of Wade Hampton III and Margaret Preston Hampton.

Caroline Louisa Hampton (1828-1902) Caroline nursed her sister-in-law Sally Baxter Hampton in her final illness in 1862. After the battlefield death of her brother, Frank Hampton in 1863, she was named the legal guardian of Sally and Frank's four children. The youngest daughter Caroline Hampton (later Halsted) only an infant at the time was her namesake.

Mary Fisher Hampton (1833-1866) Mary Fisher's mother died shortly after her birth leaving her in the care of long term family nanny, Mauma Nellie. Later in life she became the surrogate mother for the children of Wade III and Mary Singleton McDuffie. Several of the correspondence between Wade III and Mary Fisher is in the Hampton Family Papers at the University of South Carolina.

Wade III also had two younger brothers, Kit and Frank.

Christopher FitzSimons Hampton (1821-1886) Kit as he was always called, was three years younger than Wade III and a traveling companion throughout his life. He, like his older brother was a handsome man of great hunting and fishing skills. At twenty-two he married Mary Elizabeth McCord and was widowed at twenty-five. They had one daughter, Ann Fitzsimmons Hampton who lived with her father and aunt most of her life at the Hampton plantation, Linden, in Mississippi. Kit never remarried and remained devoted to his daughter, sisters and the family children who required his management of their estates. He and his daughter Annie spent much of their summers at the Hampton hunting lodge in Cashiers NC.

Frank Hampton (1829-1863) Frank was born at the Hampton family home of Millwood the seventh child of Wade Hampton II.

Considered a very handsome man as well as a superb horseman, he participated in Jockey Clubs and racecourses throughout South Carolina. At age twenty-six he married **Sally Baxter** of New York in her home and then spent the first year of their married life at Millwood Plantation. At the death of his father in 1858, Frank received a portion of Woodlands plantation to which he added more properties, referred to as the Machines and White House. Four children were born to the marriage before Sally died of tuberculosis at Millwood. Frank had enlisted in the cavalry at the beginning of the Civil War. After his wife's death, he was commissioned as a Lieutenant in the Second South Carolina Cavalry and transferred to the Army of Northern Virginia serving under the command of his brother General Wade Hampton III.

In 1855, Wade III purchased property in Cashiers Valley, NC and built a large hunting lodge. The Hamptons operated this tract both as a hunting and fishing haven and as an experimental farm with cattle driven from the South Carolina plantation.

After the death in 1852 of Margaret Preston, Wade III married **Mary Singleton McDuffie** in 1858. Soon after the wedding, they were traveling to view the land holdings in Mississippi when he received word that his father had died unexpectedly at the Walnut Ridge Plantation in Mississippi. As the estate was divided, he assumed ownership of Walnut Ridge with brothers and sisters taking other property. Soon after this time, he and Mary McDuffie began construction on a new home called Diamond Hill near the family property in the Richland District of South Carolina.

Wade Hampton III

Sketch of Wade Hampton as Commander of the Hampton Legion, from Diary of Robert Knox Sneden in 1861

Wade Hampton Distinguishes Himself Politically And Militarily

Like his predecessors, he was educated and disciplined in skills that distinguished him as a leader both politically and militarily. His rigorous life was balanced by his classical education and the time spent in his own library. As a statesman in the South that he loved, he opposed the institution of slavery and supported the limitations on its expansion. He worked politically against secession, spending much of his time in the 1850s attempting to create a different solution to the states' right issue. He was elected to the Carolina State House in 1852 and State Senate in 1858, being termed a Union Democrat. With the onset of the Civil War, he believed solidly in the South that he cherished. He vigorously supported the War efforts when he felt that there were no other political solutions.

When War was declared in early 1861, he offered to enlist as a private in the army, but was made a colonel by Governor Pickens. Newly appointed Col. Wade Hampton advertised for 1000 volunteers to form the Hampton's Legion, comprised of six companies of infantry, four troops of cavalry and a battery of artillery, much of it at his own expense. Within a week, more men had offered for enlistment than could be used. In June Hampton assembled his troops near Columbia for organization and training, departing for Richmond in early July under the command of General Pierre G.T. Beauregard.

The Hampton Legion found its first encounter with the Union Army at the Battle of Manassas in Virginia in the summer of 1861. As the battle continued, the Legion was recognized for

Wade Hampton III

In 1862 Wade Hampton was transferred to cavalry and promoted to Brigadier General

its discipline and good administration. Col. Hampton himself was wounded when a bullet grazed his head, yet he continued leading his troops. While victory was felt this day, the war still had four more years to take its toll, including four more battle inflicted wounds suffered by General Wade Hampton III.

In June 1862, the Army of Northern Virginia was re-organized forming a cavalry division under the command of General J.E.B Stuart. Hampton readily agreed to become his senior Brigadier General.

The Hampton family, as most southern families, was greatly impacted in loss of life and limb by the Civil War. At the Battle of Brandy Station, Virginia in July 1863, Hampton's brother, Col. Frank Hampton was killed while on patrol, surprised by an entrenched enemy force. His wounds included two bullets in his stomach and a sabre wound on his head. Col. Hampton's wife Sally Baxter Hampton had died earlier in Columbia. The grieving General Hampton sent his son, Preston Hampton, to escort Frank's body to lay in state in Richmond until being sent to Columbia to be buried next to Sally's in the Trinity Churchyard. Less than two weeks later, Wade III's step grandmother, Mary Cantey Hampton died in Columbia and was also buried in Trinity Churchyard.

Who Was Wade Hampton?

After the death in May 1864 of Gen. J.E.B. Stuart, Gen. Hampton was left as the ranking cavalry commander.

As an expert horseman, a skilled swordsman and a crack shot with pistol and rifle, he was fearless in battle:

"Imagine this stalwart figure with a heavy sabre buckled around the waist, and mounted upon a large and powerful animal of excellent blood and action, but wholly 'unshowy': and a correct idea will be obtained of General Wade Hampton." —Quote by John Esten Cooke, General Stuart's Chief of Ordinance in 1862, Wellman 1949

Wade Hampton III

Mural of the Battle of Louisa Court House hanging at The Citadel

The mural titled "Battle of Louisa Court House, 1864" is displayed on the walls of the Library Museum at the Military College of South Carolina, known as The Citadel, depicting the participation of The Citadel cadets led by General Wade Hampton in this battle called Trevillian Station.

On June 11-12 General Hampton led his horsemen on a route to stop General Sheridan from destroying the railroad in northern Virginia. The two-day battle near Louisa County, Virginia referred to as the Battle of Trevillian Station was considered to be the largest and bloodiest all-cavalry battle of the Civil War, employing more than 6700 Confederate and

9200 Union soldiers. On the first day of the battle it seemed that Sheridan had succeeded in winning the control of the area around the station, along with several miles of tracks, but late in the day of June 12 the cavalry under the leadership of Hampton was able to regain control, and prevent massive destruction of the railroad.

Casualties were large, but Sheridan was driven back. It is said that Sheridan, bitter in defeat, beseeched Sherman the next year on his march through Columbia, South Carolina to:

"burn that damn Hampton's house." — Quote of General Sheridan, Meynard, 1981

In February 1865, General Sherman's troops pillaged and burned the Hampton family homes of Woodlands, Millwood and Diamond Hill near Columbia.

Of all the war escapades initiated by General Hampton, his "Beef Steak Raid" was the most imaginative. Hampton knew of a herd of 2500-3000 cattle held at a Federal supply depot at Coggins Point, VA on the south side of the James River east of Petersburg and behind Union lines.

Hampton's men were in need of nourishment and wanted that herd. He developed a plan. He led 3000 raiders to the area on September 14, 1864 and on the morning of September 16 returned with 304 prisoners, 11 wagons, and most importantly 2486 head of cattle – nearly 2 million pounds of beef – to a hungry army. Lee's men would be eating "Hampton Steaks" for weeks. It was said to be enough rations to feed 50,000 men for 40 days. The Southern press was ecstatic.

On August 11, 1864 General Wade Hampton was formally named the Chief of Cavalry for the Army of Northern Virginia under the command of General Robert E. Lee.

Wade Hampton Endures Family Tragedy

As the battles continued into 1864, Lt. Wade Hampton IV was transferred into his father's staff. His younger brother Preston was attached to General Butler in the same locations. On a rainy October morning, Preston fell from his saddle mortally wounded by an enemy bullet. His brother Wade IV dismounted to assist him and was shot in the back. General Wade Hampton was on the scene immediately and transferred his wounded son Wade IV to the hospital wagon after giving comfort to his dying son Preston whispering " my son, my son." A family tragedy for the Hamptons that was felt over the entire South and described by Mary Chestnut:

The agony of that day, it is all more than a mere man can bear.
—Chestnut, 1902

Also in a letter to General Hampton written by Varina Davis, wife of President Jefferson Davis, the situation was described:

I know of nothing in history more touching than Wade Hampton's situation at the supremist moment of his misery- when he sent one son to save the other and saw them both fall.
—Andrews, 2008

On April 9, 1865 the Civil War was concluded as General Robert E. Lee surrendered to General Ulysses S. Grant in a farmhouse in Appomattox, Virginia. After the surrender in Virginia, General Joe Johnston saw the futility of southern resistance to General William T. Sherman in North Carolina and suggested a meeting with Sherman at a location between Hillsboro and Durham, NC. A small farmhouse, Bennett Place

Drawing of Bennett Place, location of meeting attended by General Hampton

was chosen for the meetings. General Wade Hampton was there in attendance on April 16.

After numerous days of negotiations, General Johnston surrendered to General Sherman on April 26, 1865, two and a half weeks after Appomattox, essentially ending the Civil War.

General Wade Hampton released his troops and returned to his home in Columbia, SC.

A weary man of 47 who had fought long and hard for four years to win a war he had expended every effort to prevent.
— Meynard, 1981

Wade Hampton III

Wade Hampton Was Truly A Bold, Fearless Leader Of Men

Wade Hampton's actions as a superb officer and as a soldier define the essence of the man. Six feet tall and powerfully built, he had legendary strength and endurance as well as being considered a genius at battle strategy.

He was one of only two officers without previous military experience to achieve the rank of Lieutenant General in the Confederate Army. He was constantly at the forefront of battle and won the open devotion of his men, referring to him as a "born soldier."

Hampton's superb horsemanship made him a natural cavalryman. Constantly at the forefront of battle, his remarkable coolness, promptness, and practical ability shows as a leader of men in dangerous circumstances. He was wounded five times in battle, plus losing a brother and a son.

Hampton was among the most frequent and successful hand-to-hand combatants among all the general officers in American history.

— Wellman, 1949

Statue created by Frederick W. Ruckstull honoring Wade Hampton III erected in 1906 on State House grounds, Columbia, SC

Wade Hampton Renews His Spirit

The Hampton Hunting Lodge in Cashiers, NC escaped destruction during the Civil War and eventually became Wade's favorite summer retreat. He felt rejuvenated after a visit, enjoying the cool breezes and majestic mountains. It is believed that he and his family came here for an extended stay in the summer after the end of the Civil War.

With bankruptcy filed in Mississippi in 1868 after the Civil War due to both the massive loss of crops in troop movement across his plantations and his debts incurred in funding the war effort, Wade wrote to his sister, Mary Fisher Hampton:

We can live very cheaply here, why not go to the Valley? Within a few hours, you can reach Walhalla, and a great road can take you over the mountain where you will live on venison, pheasants, and trout.
—Quote by Wade Hampton, Meynard, 1981

Photograph taken in New Orleans in 1866 showing the lines of strain and tragedy

Wade Hampton III

Lush Mountain Retreats

Access To Western North Carolina

In the 1830s Wade Hampton II and later Wade III spent much time traveling, visiting plantations in Mississippi and Louisiana, hunting in Cashiers Valley and enjoying a cottage in Warm Springs (now Hot Springs) North Carolina. The cottage adjoined a popular mineral springs resort hotel on the French Broad River. The mountain travel was in part to escape South Carolina's heat, humidity and mosquitoes.

The area of western North Carolina became accessible from South Carolina via the Buncombe Turnpike in 1828. The road comprised seventy-five miles from the SC/NC state line near Greenville, SC to just north of Warm Springs, NC where it crossed the Tennessee state line. Travel on the road required payment of a toll used to fund the building and maintenance of the Turnpike. Every year large amounts of livestock and commercial interests traveled this road and its connectors from Kentucky through to Savannah and Augusta resulting in the common name of "Drover's Road." By the 1880s the road was in disrepair due to the heavy use by the stagecoaches and livestock with the final use of collected tolls relinquished to the Western North Carolina Railroad.

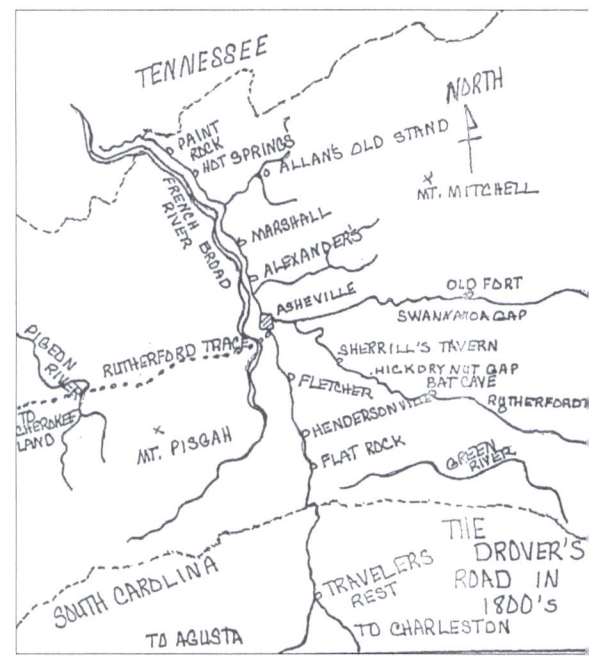

Buncombe Turnpike built in 1828 from the South Carolina state line to the Tennessee state line and often referred to as the Drover's Road

1850s saw the building of a more direct route to and from the Cashiers Valley and South Carolina called the Tuckaseegee-Keowee Turnpike providing better access for travelers from the coastal regions moving more westward. The road was built in 1857 as a joint effort between North and South Carolina, providing both access for travelers and the movement of livestock and produce to the markets in the more populated areas. The turnpike while not in existence today follows closely the State Road 107 from the Keowee River in South Carolina through Cashiers to Webster, NC.

Act passed by General Assembly for funding the Tuckaseegee-Keowee Turnpike built in 1857 from Webster, NC to the Keowee River, in SC

CHAPTER CXVIII.

AN ACT FOR THE CONSTRUCTION OF A BRIDGE ACROSS NOTLA RIVER, IN THE COUNTY OF CHEROKEE, AND FOR OTHER PURPOSES.

SECTION 1. *Be it enacted by the General Assembly of the State of North Carolina, and it is hereby enacted by the authority of the same,* That of the funds now in the hands of the Agent of the State for the collection of Cherokee Bonds, (Mr. Siler,) or may come into his hands, three thousand ($3,000) dollars shall be set apart to build the Notla Bridge, on the Western Turnpike Road, in Cherokee county, and a sufficient amount to build and repair the Macon County Turnpike Road, in Macon county, and an equal amount that it takes to build and repair the Macon County Turnpike Road shall be set apart to the Tuckaseegee and Keowee Turnpike Road, in Jackson county. To build and repair said road, the agent is hereby authorized and required to set apart said amount for the above named Bridge and Roads in bonds, designating the bonds first and second class, according to their value, and each to have an equal amount of first and second class bonds, in proportion to the amount thus set apart by the Agent, subject to the order of the President of the Company to which they belong; the appropriation for the bridge aforesaid, subject to the order of the Chairman of Cherokee County Court, and the remainder of the bonds to be applied to the Tuckaseegee and Keowee Turnpike Road, in Jackson county, the Agent paying the full amount of the contracts now let on said Road, upon the order of the President of the Company.

Cherokee bonds appropriated.

SEC. 2. *Be it further enacted,* That after the aforesaid Roads and Bridges are repaired, and complete, any funds remaining in the hands of the Agents of the State, for the collection of Cherokee bonds, or may come into their hands from the entry of vacant lands, shall be applied to works of internal improvement in the county in which said lands are situated, and the said Agents are hereby authorized to pay the same to the order of the Chairman of the several County Courts.

Disposition of remaining funds.

SEC. 3. *Be it further enacted,* That this Act shall be in force from and after its ratification.

Ratified the 21st day of December, A. D., 1866.

Wade Hampton III

*Cashiers is located in a plateau of green in
the center of mountain ranges*

Cashiers, NC
A Summer Retreat

Where Is Cashiers?

Cashiers, North Carolina today is a lovely village located on the east slope of the Eastern Continental Divide, 3487 feet above sea level in a lush valley of the highest plateau in the Blue Ridge Mountains. Cashiers is home to approximately 2000 full time residents with the addition of 35,000 seasonal guests. The valley is bounded on the north by Sheep Cliff Mountain, the backbone of the Blue Ridge, on the east by Rock Mountain and Chimneytop, on the south by the Terrapin, and on the west by the great Whiteside Mountain.

Cashiers is comparatively level, and the tourist could imaging he was in a champagne country, but for those huge domes that stand like grim sentinels encircling the valley, and upon every hand an eye of taste could select the most charming spots for residence. — Sloan 1891

The valley was a part of the Cherokee Nation lands, keeping it isolated and wild, while the Eastern U.S. coastal area was developing rapidly.

Following the treaty in 1819 between the Cherokee Nation and the United States, the land was given to the state of North

Carolina to be surveyed for homesteading by U.S. settlers. The land usable for building or farming was divided into parcels ready to be purchased as land grants by people willing to develop and live there. In the mid 1820s the Barak Norton family had received land grants from the state of North Carolina and had begun farming in the nearby area of Whiteside Cove. The Col. John Alexander Zachary family, including thirteen of his fourteen children, from Surry County, NC acquired land grants for the price of five cents an acre and began construction of a home in spring of 1833. Along with the James McKinney family from Pickens, SC they became the valley's earliest settlers, claiming land between the Chattooga River and the mountains of Chimneytop and Rock Mountain.

Other pioneers included the Allison, Alley and Bryson families. By the 1850 census there were fifteen families and ninety persons listed. Records show that in 1851 a new county named Jackson was formed by dividing the old Macon County. While the community was growing with a prospering marketplace for bartering farm products, it was still a hunting and fishing haven for the locals and the travelers staying in the boarding houses.

The post office was opened at Cashiers Valley on November 7, 1839. By 1891 the name had been officially shortened to Cashiers.

In choosing which of the many speculations of the real origin of the name, "Cashiers Valley," the post office connection is probably the most accurate. The reason for naming the community had already taken place when the post office was opened and any other confusion of how or spelling after that date would be misguided. Since there was already an active gold mine being worked in the Fairfield (now Sapphire) area, it is possible that Cashiers Valley referred to the place where

... earth and sky seem to kiss

United States Mints' assessors (or cashiers) came to exchange gold dust and nuggets into United States currency. In 1839 there were U.S. mints in Charlotte, North Carolina and Dahlonega, Georgia for production of gold coins from the gold dust and nuggets.

In 1891, a Georgian, Dave U. Sloan in his book *Fogy Days, and Now*, described this land effusively:

The visitor, in ascending this mountain region, notices the wonderful change in the atmosphere, its bracing effect on the system, the feeling of freshness and delight ... the effect on the appetite is remarkable, first keen, then ravenous. ... to describe this romantic region would require the pen of a genius and many books, after all, would have to be seen to be appreciated ... earth and sky seem to kiss.

*John C. Calhoun, noted South Carolinian
and frequent traveler with Wade Hampton*

*Mr. Calhoun made frequent visits to these mountains with
my father, examining topography of the country in view of
a railroad crossing the Blue Ridge, and could be seen
cracking rocks in search of minerals.*
—Sloan, 1891

Cashiers Valley Early Visitors

Wade III may have frequently visited Cashiers Valley, North Carolina area between the 1830s and 1850s staying in Mrs. McKinney's boarding house along with his friend, John C. Calhoun, a fellow South Carolinian and the other South Carolina honoree in Statuary Hall of the U.S. Capitol. Some of the gentleman visitors to the area were involved in business activities such as surveying for a possible railroad to connect Charleston to Knoxville, developing the turnpike road to the North Carolina line, and gold mine speculation, as well as the recreational hunting and fishing pleasures.

One of the known visitors who most likely traveled with Wade Hampton III was John C. Calhoun from South Carolina.

John C. Calhoun (1782-1850) was a U.S. Congressman, Secretary of State, Secretary of War, Vice President of the U.S. to both John Quincy Adams and Andrew Jackson, and U.S. Senator from the state of South Carolina. He was born in the Abbeville District, the third son of Patrick Calhoun, an upcountry planter, and Martha Caldwell. He entered Yale College at age 20 and graduated Phi Beta Kappa in two years. After studying law in Connecticut, he was admitted to the South Carolina Bar in 1807, but soon changed careers into politics becoming a SC State Representative and then U.S. Congressman in 1810.

Calhoun married his second cousin **Floride Bonneau Calhoun** in 1811 and had ten children (seven living to maturity.) The Calhouns lived at her family home, Fort Hill, a mansion built in 1803 including 1300 acres of property. Upon the death of her mother, Mrs. Calhoun became the owner of Fort Hill.

Calhoun "was a public intellectual of the highest order, and a uniquely gifted American politician." As South Carolina's political leader from 1824-1850, he was an original thinker, elegant speaker, and symbol of the old South. He remained steadfast on states' rights, including the right to nullify a Federal law or the right to secede from the Union. He died of tuberculosis in March of 1850 and was buried in Charleston, SC. At the death of Mrs. Calhoun in 1866, Fort Hill was then transferred to their daughter, **Anna Mariah Calhoun Clemson**.

Anna Mariah Clemson's husband was **Thomas Green Clemson** (1807-1888), an engineer, agriculturist, statesman, and high-ranking diplomat to Belgium. In 1872 they moved into Fort Hill and at his death, willed that Fort Hill "shall always be open for the inspection of visitors." The property was donated to the state of South Carolina to create an agricultural college, which became Clemson University in Clemson, SC.

There is a well recounted story told of John Calhoun stopping at a mountain cabin on the way to Mrs. McKinney's boarding house in Cashiers Valley:

There was but one spare room, and in it a bed and a pallet. My father (Col. Wm. Sloan) arranged for himself and Col. Gadsden to take the pallet and Mr. Calhoun to take the bed. About midnight the mail-rider stopped in and seeing but one person in the bed, said: 'Git furder thar; old horse and spoon,' and familiarly piled in with the Senator. —Sloan, 1891

COL. WILLIAM SLOAN.

Zachary-Tolbert home was built in the Greek Revival style similar to the Millwood House

📷 Wade Hampton The Popular Visitor

Also there are stories about Wade III and Mordecai Zachary, one of the sons of Col. John A. Zachary, the first settler of Cashiers Valley. One claim is that Wade III lent Mordecai money for building his boarding house in 1842 in return for letting Hampton board for free. This historic construction of the Zachary-Tolbert House reflects the influence of the Greek-Revival style from the South Carolina Low Country. The Zachary-Tolbert House was placed on the National Register of Historic Places and is now the home to the Cashiers Historical Society.

Another fellow South Carolinian traveler to Cashiers was Armistead Burt (1802-1883) a prominent lawyer and politician from Abbeville, SC. He was a protégé, disciple, and nephew by marriage to John C. Calhoun. As a U.S. Congressman (1843-1853) he was Speaker of the House and spent much time in Washington. He also had the responsibility of taking care of Senator Calhoun during his long illness.

Burt was also a good friend to Jefferson Davis, the President of the Confederacy. The Civil War effectively ended in Burt's Abbeville home when Davis' last meeting of his Confederacy War Cabinet was held there in May, 1865.

As Wade Hampton's lawyer, financial mentor and confidant, they spent time together in Cashiers, as well as in South Carolina. Burt bought the Zachary-Tolbert Home as his summer home in 1873 and remained there until 1881. In the gubernatorial election of 1876, Burt was politically instrumental in getting Hampton elected as South Carolina's famed, first Reconstruction Governor.

From his home in Abbeville, Burt corresponded with his many prominent South Carolinian friends, connecting political and social interests. He invited many of them to his Cashiers Valley summer retreat, including Thomas Green Clemson, the founder of Clemson University.

Middle of Cashiers in 1920....
Geneva Zachary, mother of author Jane Nardy, at her grandfather's house
on Rt. 107, with Whiteside mountain in view

Jackson County recorded deed refers to Alexander Zachary
selling land to Wade Hampton in 1855.

Wade Hampton III

Land Deed

...ree with myself my heirs and assigns to warrant and defend the title of said land against all other claims the same.

Test Charles Woodring }   his
Henry Brown   }   James x Hooper (seal)
                 mark

State of North Carolina } The execution of the within Deed was duly proven before me by
Jackson County   } the oath of H. L. Brown one of the subscribing witnesses, thereto, let it be registered in Jackson County. Certified August 24th. A. D. 1855.
                D. Rogers C. C. Clk.
            Witness Wm. R. Buchanan R. J. C.

   This Indenture made the twenty fourth day of September in the year one thousand eight hundred and fifty five between Alexander Zachary of Cashiers Valley in the County of Jackson and State of North Carolina of the first part and John S. Preston, Wade Hampton and C. S. Hampton of Richland District South Carolina of the second part. Witnesseth that the said party of the first part for and in consideration of the sum of seventy two dollars & fifty cents lawful money of the United States to him duly paid before the delivery hereof hath bargained and sold and by these presents doth grant and convey to the said parties of the second part, their heirs and assigns forever, all that certain piece and parcel of land lying and being in Cashiers Valley Jackson County North Carolina and which is known and described as follows, towit commencing at a Spannish Oak Stump corner of William Norton's land, and running S. 76° W. thirty two poles to a Spannish Oak; then South 2 West sixty four poles to a White Oak; then East thirty six poles to a Hickory thence North eighteen poles to another corner of William Norton's land, and from thence North back fifty eight poles to a Spannish Oak stump, said tract or parcel of Land containing according the survey Jefferson Zachary made the twenty seventh day of September A. D. 1855 fourteen one half acres, together with all and singular the tenements hereditaments and appurtenances and all the estate title and interes of the said party of the first part therein. And the said party of the first part doth hereby covenant and agree with the said party of the second part, that at the time of the delivery hereof the said party of the first part is the legal owner of the premises above granted and seized and seized thereof in fee simple absolute, and that he will warrant and defend the above granted premises in the quiet and peaceable possession of the said party of the second part their heirs and assigns forever. In testimony whereof I have hereunto set my hand and seal this twenty fourth day of September one thousand eight hundred and fifty five.

In presents of M. Zachary }   Alexander Zachary (seal)
      W. Zachary }

State of North Carolina } The execution of the foregoing Deed was duly proven before
Jackson County   } me by the oath of W. Zachary one of the subscribing witnesses thereto recorded. Let it be registered in Jackson County.
      Certified October 10th. 1855.   D. Rogers C. C. Clk.
         Witness Wm. R. Buchanan R. J. C.

Wade Hampton The Cashiers Land Owner

The confirmation of the dates of land purchased by Wade Hampton and his family required a search of recorded deeds in both Macon and Jackson Counties, North Carolina. As a dedicated historian, the author Jane Nardy researched in 2006 all of the written records of both counties as well as accessible family letters at the South Caroliniana Library.

In 1845 Cashiers Valley was a part of Macon County, as Jackson County was not formed until 1851. Both counties have complete, extant deed books, which do not list any Hampton land purchases in Cashiers when it was part of Macon County. In the Jackson County deed book two deeds were recorded that reflect the purchase of property by Wade Hampton III and two family members who jointly purchased property in Cashiers Valley in 1855.

September 24, 1855, two parcels of land were sold to Wade Hampton III, John S. Preston (Wade III's brother-in-law), and Christopher F. Hampton (Wade III's brother, Kit).

1. 14 ½ acres from Alexander Zachary for $72.50
2. 23 ¼ acres for $116.25 from William Norton (brother-in-law of Alexander Zachary)

Less than two months later, the same trio from Richland District, South Carolina purchased additional land.

3. 364 acres adjoining the first parcels for $2,000 from Woodford Zachary (brother of Alexander Zachary)

The three land sales in 1855 totaled approximately 400 acres at an average cost of $5.25 per acre.

Wade Hampton III

Wade Hampton Hunting Lodge built circa 1856

Wade Hampton The Retreat Builder

Wade Hampton III with his brother Kit Hampton came to this lush valley of North Carolina in search of recreational activities, escaping the heat and malaria prone summers of South Carolina and Mississippi. The Hamptons were attracted to the beauty and exquisite landscape of Cashiers Valley, describing it as a "paradise."

During his visits he greatly influenced the region in what was then the frontier in western North Carolina. He customarily made the trek with a substantial entourage from South Carolina to his family's seven-bedroom mountain home, referred to as the Hampton Hunting Lodge. The hunting lodge may have been built with the help of Mordecai Zachary. The cabin was located on the property, which today is a part of the popular High Hampton Inn. Soon after the purchase, the Hamptons operated the tract both as a hunting preserve and an experimental farm, driving a herd of prize cattle with them. The original hunting lodge stood on the property until the Inn burned in May 1932, and was not rebuilt.

The Cashiers Valley abounded with bear, deer, and small game. Hunting was Wade III's favorite pastime with both gun and knife. He is credited with killing numerous bear with only a knife. Wade Hampton was also an avid fisherman and was praised for stocking the rivers and streams with trout each year upon his arrival at the lodge. There are stories told about him carrying fingerlings in buckets from the streams on the western side of the Continental Divide to his favorite haunts on the eastern side.

One story of a successful deer hunt was memorialized in a poem sent to Wade Hampton in the early 1890s.

Last Hunt with Hampton

*But Summer's past and Fall has come,
Now turn our thoughts to going home.
Here's a yarn, some may call it luck,
Col. Hampton wished a deer-a buck.*

*A whole buck to his home to take,
So we did the arrangement make:
Take to Columbia on his return,
He'll testify to the whole concern.*

......

*And fell dead (the buck) within twenty rods,
That shot was worthy of the gods;
Wagon was waiting at the road,
That buck made part of the Colonel's load.*

......

*Of the best timber was he made,
And braver ne'er donned the plaid;
Nature's nobleman, luck or adversity,
The hero be known to posterity.*
—Sloan, 1891

Wade Hampton wrote back to D. U. Sloan after receiving this poem in April, 1891, apologizing first for the delay in responding and then remarking on the changes.

……..I remember well the incident you refer to as I do many pleasant hours spent with you in the mountains of North Carolina.

There have been many changes since those and many of them for the worst, but I hope that our South may yet be prosperous.

With kind regard I am,
Very truly yours,
Wade Hampton
      —Sloan, 1891

OR, THE WORLD HAS CHANGED.

I remember well the incident you refer to, as I do many pleasant hours spent with you in the mountains of North Carolina. There have been many changes since those days, and many of them for the worst, but I hope that our South may yet be prosperous. With my kind regards I am,

    Very truly yours,   WADE HAMPTON.

P. S.—Two or three years ago I shot a buck here which weighed with entrals out 265 pounds; his skin, from neck to end of tail, is seven feet long. I have here, too, a pair of horns with twenty-eight points.   H.

To D. U. Sloan, Atlanta, Ga.

Wade Hampton III

Cashiers Valley
August 8, 1859

My Dear Manning

Letter is in collection of author Bob Lathan

Yours truly
W. Hampton

Wade Hampton The Letter Writer

There are a few known letters from Wade III to his sister, Mary Fisher and to a friend, Manning with references to his favorable experiences in Cashiers Valley that are dated 1857 and 1859, respectively, after his 1855 land purchases.

John Laurence Manning (1816-1889) was a planter, soldier and politician. He attended Princeton University and graduated from South Carolina College. In 1838 he married **Susan Frances Hampton**, the youngest child of Wade Hampton I and Mary Cantey Hampton. They built the Milford Plantation near Pinewood, Clarendon County, SC, which was built by the same architect, Nathaniel Potter of Rhode Island who designed the Hampton family home, Millwood. Considered one of the finest examples of Greek Revival architecture, it was placed on the National Registry of Historic Places in 1971.

Manning served as Governor of South Carolina from 1852-1854. He and Wade Hampton III were close friends, and political associates throughout their lives.

Wade Hampton The Strategic Planner

Many stories are told of the activities of Wade Hampton in the Cashiers Valley Hunting Lodge, but it is sure that he continued to entertain friends and conclude business while enjoying the cool summers and relaxed surroundings. During the years immediately after the War, Hampton filed for bankruptcy in Jackson, MS, and later founded the Southern Life Insurance Company in Atlanta with General John B. Gordon and Benjamin H. Hill. He was also Vice President of the Carolina Life Insurance Company.

In 1872 the Amnesty Act was passed by the U.S. Congress restoring voting and election rights to the officers who had served in the Confederate Army, including General Wade Hampton. While certainly a significant challenge, Wade Hampton III was then given the opportunity to serve his state of South Carolina in an elected position.

One very plausible activity that has been reported to have taken place in Cashiers is his consultation with his brother Kit as to the possibility of standing for this party's nomination for the South Carolina governorship. Even with his personal extensive popularity throughout South Carolina, it would be a race against great odds of winning. The Hampton brothers spent time at the lodge weighing the decision and choosing that Wade III should run.

Wade Hampton Leads Again

While a hard fought election and a protracted fight to assume control of the governorship, in April 1876, Wade Hampton III became the first Governor of South Carolina after Reconstruction.

He was re-elected easily on November 6, 1878. The morning following the election he decided to join friends on a deer hunt in lower Richland County. Arriving late to the hunt, Wade could not find a horse, so took a servant's mule. Some distance into the brush he saw a deer, fired the gun and the deer fell dead. Wade dismounted but landed off balance and suffered a compound fracture of his lower leg. Because he lay unattended for a long time, the wound became infected. After a long struggle, being nursed constantly in his home in Columbia, the doctors decided to amputate his lower leg, which did save his life. During the time of his extreme illness, he both resigned the governorship and was elected by the legislature to serve as U.S. Senator beginning in March 1879 for the next twelve years. The legend in Washington was that he had a cork leg.

Wade Hampton III had many positions during his life: planter, plantation owner, businessman, legislator, community leader, soldier, governor and senator.

Wade Hampton's election triumph

Wade Hampton III

Whether one liked him or not, one was impressed by him. Not only was he of a heroic size and dignified bearing, but his behavior was so courtly as to be pattern for all the meticulous South. —Wellman, 1949

During his final service as senator from South Carolina, Hampton fought hard against the passage of the Force Bill, which was an act to provide Federal overseers at the polling booths to ensure the qualifications of all voters. Hampton's last speech to the Senate, and most likely his last speech as an elected official, was regarded as one of his best and wished by many that could have been heard by all Americans. After his forceful speech the Bill was dropped from the agenda of the U.S. Senate.

"When you intrude upon the rights of any citizen in the exercise of his Constitutional and lawful expression in national affairs, you intrude upon the rights of every American citizen and of every free State."
—Quote of Senator Wade Hampton, Wellman, 1949

Photograph of Senator Wade Hampton taken in Washington, DC in late 1880s

Wade Hampton Community Benefactor

Throughout his life Wade Hampton was admired by North Carolinians, just as the South Carolinians. Wade Hampton's commitments and joys in sharing the hunting lodge and the Cashiers Valley with family and friends continued throughout his active life. His strong leadership, energetic mind, and outdoor activities made recognizable marks of positive lasting impact.

In 1878, Reverend John Deal, with the help of Wade Hampton III and three of his sisters, founded a mission church in Cashiers Valley and named it the Good Shepherd. During the summers for several years, Sunday services were conducted in the Hampton's one room schoolhouse, which was the same place the Methodist Church held their services. It was not unusual for several church denominations to share the same building.

When that schoolhouse where Reverend Deal preached burned, funds were raised to build a real church, completed in 1886. Unfortunately, the building burned eight years later. Undaunted by fires, building started again and a new church was dedicated in 1895.

At her death in 1910, Miss Kate Hampton, sister of Wade Hampton III left a bequest of 150 acres of land adjoining the Millwood property as an endowment to the well being of this church in Cashiers.

Church of the Good Shepherd built by Hampton family in Cashiers, NC

This present Church of the Good Shepherd is an Episcopal Church of the Diocese of Western North Carolina. It occupies prominent geography across the road from the entrance to High Hampton Inn and is the oldest church structure in Cashiers. The lovely small church has stained glass windows and a small cemetery. The magnificent bronze bell beside the church was cast for the Hamptons in 1892 by the McShane Foundry in Baltimore, Maryland. The bell had a long journey by sea to Charleston and then on a wagon the rest of the way to its final destination adjacent to the Church. The wooden tower was

Jewel Lake built by the Hamptons in the 1850s for the production of ice

replaced in 2002 with new cypress beams and iron supports for the legs. Ironwood was used for the platform for the bell. The bell still welcomes visitors to the Valley today.

Activities abounded around the hunting lodge that included the Hamptons building of the lake for fishing, swimming, and for the production of ice. From the frozen Jewel Lake in the winter, ice blocks were cut and stored for use in the summer in the preservation of food as well as the beverages served. The favorite of Wade Hampton and his guests was the mint julep, using crushed ice from the lake.

Cabin built by the Hamptons in 1870s served as a schoolhouse for the Cashiers families

So many local Cashiers Valley families were involved that a separate cabin, probably built in the early 1870s near the hunting lodge, served as a schoolhouse for local children and for Methodist Sunday on the weekends. The cabin is used today as a guest cottage at High Hampton Inn.

The name of Wade Hampton lives on today through the continued enjoyment of cool and restful mountain retreat of the High Hampton Inn.

High Hampton Inn, the popular mountain retreat

The inn was built on the original site of the Hampton Hunting Lodge, which burned in 1932.

Wade Hampton III

*"Honeymoon cottage" on
Jewel Lake at High Hampton Inn*

Wade Hampton is honored for his contributions to the Cashiers community

Buncombe Turnpike called the Drover's Road connected South Carolina to the Tennessee line through Warm Springs

Warm Springs, NC an Accessible Retreat

Where Is Warm/Hot Springs?

Another site that the Hamptons definitely visited was Warm Springs, North Carolina located on the French Broad River, northwest of Asheville near the border with Tennessee. The natural hot mineral springs were discovered in 1778 by a group of mountaineer white settlers with evidence that the Cherokee had used the springs and believed in their curative powers. In 1791 a tavern owned by William Nelson prospered and help to establish the springs as a respite of great importance.

In 1828, the Buncombe Turnpike, seventy-five miles long, was completed along the French Broad River, through Warm Springs, connecting Tennessee and Kentucky to the east coast. It was the superhighway of the South at that time, also known as the "Drover's Road." Farmers drove thousands of hogs, cattle, horses, turkeys and other livestock on the turnpike from Tennessee and Kentucky to markets in Charleston and Augusta and stopping at Warm Springs, along the way, for the waters.

The main crop of the mountaineers was corn, and the best way to market it was by feeding it to hogs, large cows, and turkeys. In the late fall, the roads were alive with livestock for the trip to the markets. The drovers relied on helpers, usually young boys, to keep the animals moving by cracking whips tied with strips of red flannel. Hogs, the most numerous animals on the turnpike, could only travel six to eight miles a day. It was estimated that over 150,000 hogs passed through Asheville each October to December, bringing prosperity to Buncombe County, but also contributing to the decay of the road.

Stagecoaches also began using the turnpike shortly after it opened and ran on regular schedule from Charleston to Greenville, South Carolina and from there to Asheville and on to Tennessee. The availability of the turnpike and stagecoach would have made it relatively easy for the Hamptons to travel from South Carolina to Warm Springs, North Carolina.

350 room Warm Springs Hotel opened in the 1830s

In the 1830s James Patton of Asheville, NC bought the Springs and with his two sons opened the 350-room Warm Springs Hotel. The hotel was built with thirteen grand columns, commemorating the original colonies and included a dining room to seat 600. Zebulon B. Vance, who later became the Civil War governor of North Carolina, worked as a clerk in the hotel.

It became a very popular spa and retreat that was accessible by the turnpike, with surroundings that were mountainous, heavily wooded, and teeming with game. It is believed that Wade Hampton II frequently visited the hotel and stayed in a cottage on the grounds bringing his family for portions of their summer retreat from the South Carolina heat:

in the 1830s Wade Hampton built a summer cottage as a part of the hotel. —Painter, 1992

New Owners, New Name

In 1862, James H. Rumbough, from Greeneville, Tennessee, bought the Warm Springs Hotel and settled his family into the Hampton Cottage before joining the Confederate Army. After the War, the hotel became increasing popular with travelers and journalists from all over the country. The hotel burned in 1884 and Rumbough sold "the rubble" to a syndicate of northern investors.

In 1886 the investors not only built a new hotel called the Mountain Park Hotel, but discovered a new spring with waters of 104 degrees, and changed the town's name to Hot Springs. The Mountain Park was one of the elegant resorts in the country, consisting of a 200-room hotel, a farm and stables, the first golf course in North Carolina, a bath house over the sixteen marble pools, and the Hampton Cottage all sitting upon landscaped acres.

Through the years the hotel ownership changed several times, each time resulting in a new Rumbough family member assuming management.

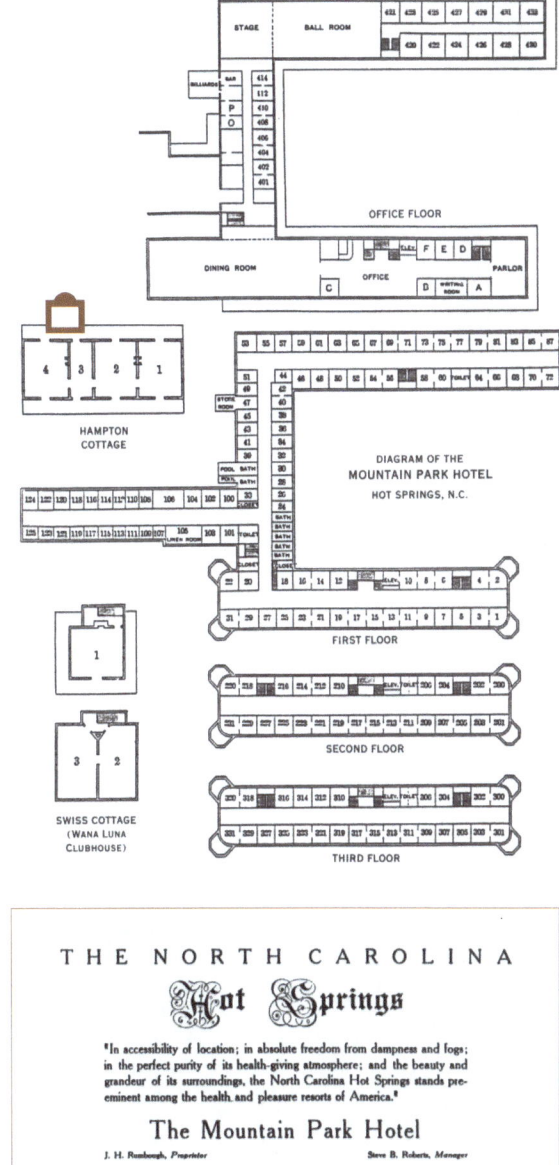

Hampton Family Influences Hot Springs Decision

In 1917 the hotel was leased by James Edwin Rumbough to the United States Government as an internment camp for over 2,000 enemy aliens who had been quartered in immigrant centers. These were German merchant sailors captured in U.S. harbors, when the US entered WWI. The Germans had been in N.Y. Harbor in luxury liners and were moved south by train to Hot Springs. The internees were treated well by the townspeople.

National news reporters, also visited Hot Springs, since it held more aliens than the three other American internment camps. This included a large panoramic photo in the New York Times in November 1917 of the 'German Prisoners Enjoying Life in Uncle Sam's Care on the Beautiful Grounds of the Internment Camp at Hot Springs, NC.' It was clearly hoped that reciprocal treatment would be given Americans on German soil.
—Painter, 1992 and Ron Rash, 2012

The Hampton Cottage, for a period of time, was used as a camp hospital during the German invasion of 1917. Later that year a new hospital was finished in the internment camp:

giving great improvement over little Hampton Cottage, and insuring better health care for the Germans. —Painter, 1992

It is somewhat ironic that Alfred Hampton, the youngest son of Wade Hampton III, was the person who suggested that the Mountain Park Hotel should be the site of the internment camp of 2,000 Germans.

Alfred Hampton (1863-1942) was the eighth child of Wade Hampton III. He was educated at the University of Virginia and worked as a civil engineer until the beginning of the Spanish American War. He joined the command of Gen. M.C.Butler, one of his father's former cavalry officers from the Civil War and served at San Juan Hill. In 1909 he was employed by the Federal Bureau of Immigration until joining President Woodrow Wilson's cabinet as Director of Prisoner of War Camps during WWI.

It was Alfred Hampton, grandson of Wade Hampton (II), well acquainted with Hot Springs, and connected with the Department of Labor, who had suggested the Mountain Park Hotel and grounds for the camp.
—Asheville *Citizen-Times,* Painter, 1992.

In his responsibilities as director of Prisoners of War, Alfred Hampton continued to visit the camp and make written reports on its administration.

Cottage built and enjoyed by the Hamptons on the hotel property

The Hampton Cottage is no longer standing. In 1920, the elegant hotel burned and ended an era of the fancy resort life. A smaller Hot Springs Inn was built, but later burned in 1977 and Hot Springs fell into decline.

Today, Hot Springs, NC is a special place of beauty and relaxation. The grounds of the hotel have become a 100 acre Hot Springs Resort and Spa with a campground, mineral baths, and relaxation therapies. The 2,100-mile Appalachian Trail runs down the main street of town before crossing the French Broad River. Hikers, rafters, and mountain bikers can certainly explore the scenery there and soak in the hot mineral baths.

Hot Springs, NC. A modern outdoor recreation destination with the confluence of the French Broad River and Spring Creek providing the water sports. The hiking trails, including the Appalachian Trail, abound with the mountain ranges and Pisgah National Forest.

Hot Springs, NC honors a Hampton contribution

Wade Hampton III

Wade Hampton on porch of his home

Wade Hampton Beloved Gentleman

His elected positions completed Wade Hampton returned to Columbia and to his mountain retreat. In 1893 at the age of seventy-five he accepted the U.S. Cabinet position of Railroad Commissioner under President Cleveland, traveling throughout the U.S. for five years.

In the spring of 1899, the Hampton family suffered another loss due to fire as arsonists burned the houses at Millwood and Southern Cross. He lost most of his household belongs, saving his swords and family silver. Temporarily he and his daughter, **Mary Singleton Hampton** (1861-1934) known as Daisy moved into the caretaker's cabin at Diamond Hill. He could not afford another house, but the people of Columbia raised funds through the state to build a residence at the corner of Barnwell and Senate streets. Wade Hampton secured ads in the local newspapers requesting people not to contribute, but they did so anyway.

The house was completed in 1901 and presented to him on his 83rd birthday. He and Daisy stayed in the house until his death.

Southern Cross home burned in 1899

As his health began to deteriorate, the family gathered in his last days of April 1902 to hear him remember times of years previous. His youngest son, Alfred recorded Hampton's nourishment and his last words,

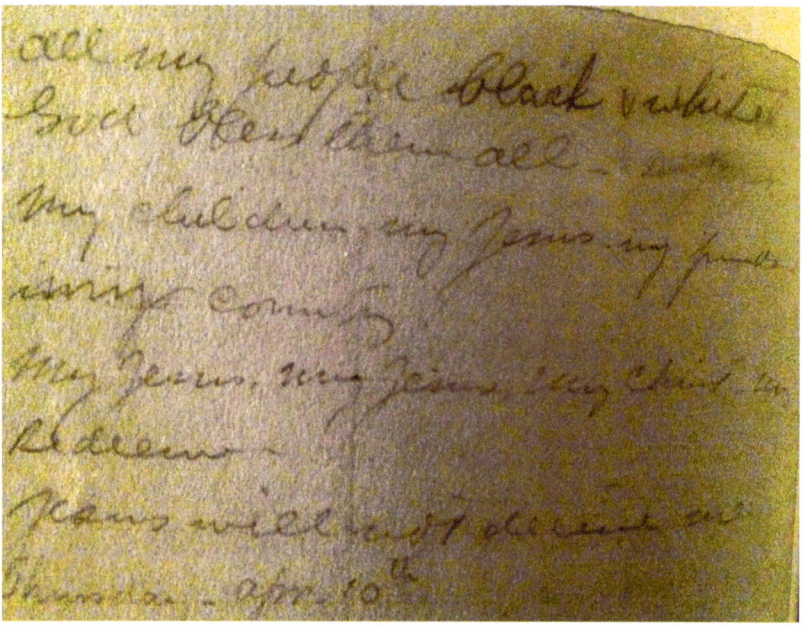

... all my people, black and white. God bless them all.
—Wade Hampton III

His funeral was the largest in time in South Carolina. Twenty thousand mourners, black and white, lined the streets of Columbia. Wade Hampton III was buried in Columbia in the Trinity Churchyard, among the graves of his ancestors, children, and siblings, leaving an imposing legacy, which spread from Louisiana, through the Carolinas to the U.S. Capitol.

Hampton Traditions Continue

The Aunties Take Responsibility

In 1863 at the death of Col. Frank Hampton, (1829-1863), Wade III's younger brother, during the Civil War, his four small children were left in the care of Aunt Caroline and the other Aunties at the Woodlands plantation.

Sally Baxter (1833-1862) Sally was descended from early settlers of New England. Her mother was connected with John Quincy Adams. She was known to have many friends and admirers, including William Makepeace Thackeray. In 1855 she and Frank Hampton were married at the home of her family in New York City. She and Frank moved to Woodlands soon after the wedding until the beginning of the Civil War when they moved to Charleston to be near his military assignment. Sally died at Woodlands in 1862 of tuberculosis after a long illness. The children stayed with the Aunties at Woodlands awaiting the return of their father.

Sally Baxter, mother of Caroline Hampton Halsted

At the death of Frank, Christopher Hampton was appointed administrator and set about immediately selling assets to provide for the children and their guardian, Miss Caroline Hampton. Georgia Anna and Lucy went to live in New York with the Baxters. while Franky, Jr and baby Caroline stayed at Millwood.

Who Was Caroline Hampton Halsted?

Frank Hampton, father of Caroline Hampton Halsted

Caroline Hampton (1861-1922) was born at the Hampton family home of Woodlands. With the early death of her parents, and the burning of the Woodlands, and Millwood plantations, she and her brother were raised by her unmarried aunts, in a home near the burned ruins of Millwood. She attended school with her sister at Miss Randolph's in Virginia. In 1885 Caroline entered nursing school in New York City, graduating from New York Hospital in 1888. When the Johns Hopkins Hospital opened in 1889, she moved to Baltimore and was appointed chief nurse of the operating room by the famous surgeon Dr. William Halsted.

Caroline became Dr. Halsted's scrub nurse in surgery, but developed severe contact dermatitis in 1889, as her sensitive hands could not tolerate the disinfectants of mercuric chloride and carbolic acid (phenol). Halsted requested the Goodyear Rubber Company to make two pairs of rubber gloves to protect her hands. This marked the beginning of the use of rubber gloves in the operating room in this country with Caroline Hampton the first person to use them.

Even with the busy political schedule as governor and later senator, Wade Hampton and the family continued to gather

Caroline Hampton, chief nurse of the operating room at Johns Hopkins Hospital

in Cashiers Valley in the summer. The train was taken from Columbia to Walhalla and from there up the mountain by other conveyance. After Wade's sisters, the Aunties, Kate, Ann and Caroline became the owners of the property, they continued to share with many offsprings of the Hampton clan.

In 1890, Caroline Hampton, the niece of Wade Hampton III married Dr. William Halsted at her home at Millwood. The newly married Halsteds spent their honeymoon in the Cashiers Hampton Hunting Lodge.

William Stewart Halsted, M.D. (1852-1922) was considered one of the greatest and most influential surgeons of all time. He was born in New York City and graduated from Yale University and the Columbia University College of Physicians. After studying for two years in Europe, he was in the private practice of surgery in New York.

In 1889, the new hospital and medical school opened in Baltimore as Johns Hopkins with Dr. Halsted named as surgeon in chief and the first professor of surgery. Halsted is credited with starting the first surgical residency training programs in the U.S. as well as many state of the art surgical procedures. Halsted's innovations and contributions to surgery include the following:

- As a medical student, invented a traction apparatus for neck fractures.
- As a resident was also responsible for the inclusion of temperature charts in the medical record.
- In 1881, performed the first emergency blood transfusion (on his sister) and one of the first operations for gallstones (on his mother).
- Was the first to use cocaine for local and regional anesthesia and the also the first to demonstrate spinal anesthesia. This discovery greatly enlarged the scope of dentistry.
- Was the first to promote "safe surgery" (asepsis, careful handling of tissues, hemostasis, and introduction of fine silk sutures and delicate forceps).
- Developed new operations for intestinal, stomach, gallbladder, thyroid, hernia, and breast surgery. Also signaled advances in vascular surgery.
- Promoted rubber glove for scrub nurse Caroline.

Portrait of William Stewart Halsted

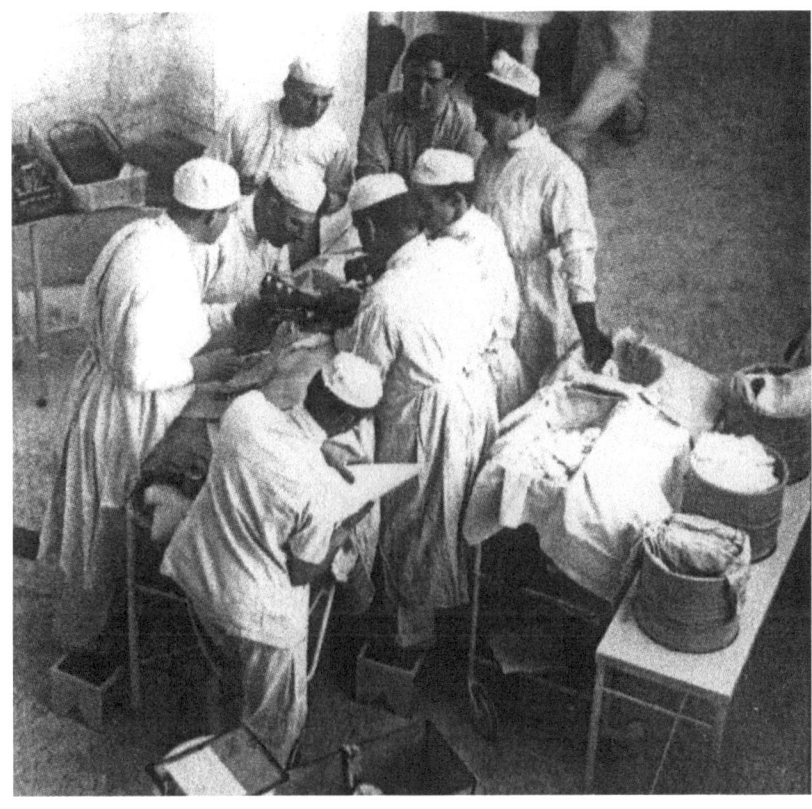

Surgical Suite at Johns Hopkins Hospital with Dr. Halsted as Chief Surgeon

- Was the first to use plate and screw techniques with burial screws for long bone fractures.
- Most importantly, was the first in the USA to develop a "school of surgery": a rigorous training program for young surgeons. His department of surgery established four subspecialties: otolaryngology, urology, orthopedics, and neurosurgery.

Not only did Dr. Halsted become one of the greatest surgeons of all times, he also became Caroline's partner in continuing the Hampton tradition of developing land and gardens.

Halsted enjoyed his months in their family retreat

After honeymooning in Cashiers at the Hampton Lodge, Dr. Halsted purchased the 400 acre-plus property in 1892 from his wife's three Hampton aunts and renamed it "High Hampton" as a combination name of his family estate in England, "High Halsted" and her family in the Carolinas. Halsted became enthralled with the beauty of the property and realized it

would be a retreat from the heat and humidity of the Baltimore summers. High Hampton was an ideal retreat for Halsted, who loved solitude. Halsted gradually bought the surrounding small farms for approximately $5 per acre, enlarging the estate to over 2,200 acres at the time of his death in 1922.

Dr. Halsted typically left Baltimore around June 1 and returned around October 1. Mrs. Halsted, who generally arrived in May and stayed until Thanksgiving, literally ran the farm and directed the hired hands, supervising the planting of the gardens and crops. She preferred the outdoor life at High Hampton to the social amenities of Baltimore. She, like her predecessors, was a skilled rider and known for her horsemanship.

Caroline Halsted loved Cashiers and spent most of her time managing their property

Dahlia garden at High Hampton Inn was created as a Halsted passion

Caroline and Halsted took a great deal of interest in their mountain neighbors who depended on Dr. Halsted for their medical needs. They respected him greatly, and he sent a good number to the Johns Hopkins Hospital, frequently paying their expenses.

At High Hampton, Caroline's days were very active. She worked in the fields from morning to night. Halsted was very proud of her farming work and wrote several letters from Baltimore giving specific comments on planting crops and purchasing animals.

As partners in Cashiers, they were well matched in their devotion to each other and to the property of the expanded High Hampton. Both were from distinguished families, but different in their personalities. She was very aristocratic,

Halsteds built their own cottage on the property

while he enjoyed solitude and was very much a perfectionist in the medical profession and in all of his activities.

While Caroline enjoyed and developed vegetable gardens, she also used her mechanical skills in building a sawmill and a system to move water uphill into the main house. Dr. Halsted found true satisfaction in finding and importing specimen trees from Europe, then meticulously planting them in prominent places such as the entrance to the property. One of his treasured activities was the development of the dahlia garden. Each year he ordered bulbs from researched distant sources and nurtured the garden as if it were a patient in his care. The beauty of the dahlia garden was shared with the community not only in viewing but each fall when the garden became too large many bulbs and flowers were provided as a gift from the Halsteds to the people in Cashiers.

Dr. Halsted died in September 1922 after complications from gall bladder surgery in Baltimore. Caroline died less than three months later with pneumonia due in part to her exhaustion over the death of her beloved partner.

In 1924, the property was sold to Lyndon McKee of Sylva, Jackson County, North Carolina. The Halsted Cottage, built by Caroline and William, burned in 1932 and was rebuilt as a part of the High Hampton Inn facilities.

While the property transfer concluded the ownership of the Hampton family, the enjoyment and caretaking of the land, and its treasures continues, including the famous dahlia garden. An historical marker in the center of Cashiers honors Hampton as its most famous summer resident. His name lives on in Cashiers with the High Hampton Inn, The Wade Hampton Golf Club, the Hampton School, and Wade Road. The spirit of the Hamptons is still powerful.

Hampton Traditions

Church of the Good Shepherd

High Hampton Inn

Porch of new Hampton cottage at High Hampton Inn

Wade Hampton Golf Club

Hampton Biographies

Wade Hampton III is the subject of many biographies. The first biography referenced in this presentation was by Manly Wade Wellman in 1949 titled *Giant in Gray*. A lengthy work on the Hampton family, *The Venturers*, by Virginia Meynard was published in 1981.

Four complete biographies have been published in the last decade. Longacre, 2003; Cisco, 2004; Ackerman, 2007; and Andrew, 2008.

Most of these biographies refer to the Hamptons purchasing their mountain land in 1845. Wellman did not mention a date of purchase but stated that "his (Wade III's) summer pleasure led him to a family property high in the mountains….called Cashiers Valley, operated as a hunting preserve…The big farmland was called High Hampton." (High Hampton) was not named until 1892 by Dr. William S. Halsted.

The Venturers, in 1981, refers to the date 1845, "It was about that time that Col. Hampton (Wade II) and his two eldest sons, Wade III, and Kit (Christopher), looking for a hunting preserve in a cool climate, jointly purchased 2,300 acres of land in Cashiers Valley, North Carolina, and built a large, rustic lodge there…a private retreat of the entire family…the Hamptons expanded and developed the Cashiers estate, which they called The Valley."

Andrew, the most recent biographer in 2008, refers to Wade Hampton III (in the late 1830s), "Every year his father took him and Kit to Mississippi to oversee (the plantations there)…

They arrived in February or early March and stayed until late April or May. After returning...to Columbia, South Carolina, they traveled north...to spend the hottest weeks of the summer in Newport, Rhode Island or, more often, at the stylish White Sulphur Springs resort in the mountains of Virginia...By November, they were back in Mississippi...(and) usually stayed there through Christmas.

Andrew also states, "Wade III's favorite pastime was hunting. He avidly hunted game around Millwood and in Mississippi. Later (date not stated), Wade II, Wade III, and Kit bought 2,300 acres in Cashiers Valley in the North Carolina mountains. Wade III's wife, Margaret, bore him his first daughter, Sally, at her parents' home in Abington, Virginia, in July 1845. Andrew follows, "That was the summer that Hampton, his father, and Kit devoted to building a mountain home and several cabins at their 2,300 acre preserve in Cashiers, North Carolina."

This information on the Hamptons' 1840s land ownership in Cashiers, North Carolina can not be confirmed by any legal sources such as deed records in North Carolina or by papers and letters in the South Caroliniana Library in Columbia, South Carolina. The archivist at the Library has confirmed that the existing papers of Wade Hampton II never mentioned Cashiers Valley and papers of Wade III made only sporadic reference to Cashiers - all from the post-Civil-War period, possibly because the earlier papers were destroyed when Hampton houses were burned by Sherman's troops.

Virginia Meynard, the author of *The Venturers* describes the meeting of heirs and division of Wade II's estate with no mention of Cashiers Valley property.

Wade Hampton III

It is known that Wade Hampton II had a special interest in White Sulphur Springs, Virginia, where he built the Colonnade in 1837 in the Greek Revival style, as a summer home to be shared by Richard Singleton. Wade III met his future wife, Margaret Preston, at the Colonnade.

Historically, the Hamptons traveled extensively. There are recorded deeds, notes and letters from many dates and many places. It is only recorded that 400 acres of land was purchased by Wade Hampton in 1855 in Cashiers Valley. However, the contributions and marks can still be seen and felt throughout Cashiers Valley.

Sources

Books

Ackerman, Robert K. *Wade Hampton III*. Columbia: University of South Carolina Press, 2007.

Andrew, Rod Jr. *Wade Hampton: Confederate Warrior to Southern Redeemer*. Chapel Hill: University of North Carolina Press, 2008.

Blethen, H. Tyler and Wood, Curtis W. Jr. *From Ulster to Carolina*. Raleigh, NC: North Carolina Office of Archives and History, 1998.

Chestnut, Mary Boykin. *A Diary from Dixie*. New York: Houghton Mifflin, 1903

Cisco, Walter Brian. *Wade Hampton: Confederate Warrior, Conservative Statesman*. Washington, DC: Brassey's, 2004.

Longacre, Edward G. *Gentlemen and Soldier: The Extraordinary Life of General Wade Hampton*. Nashville, TN: Rutledge Hill Press, 2003.

McKee, Becky. *High Hampton Inn, 90 Years of Making*. Decatur, GA: Looking Glass Books, 2012.

Meynard, Virginia G. *The Venturers: The Hampton, Harrisons, and Earle Families of Virginia, South Carolina, and Texas*. Greenwood, SC: Southern Historical Press, 1981.

Painter, Jacqueline Burgin. *The German Invasion of Western NC*. Asheville, NC: Biltmore Press, 1992.

Rash, Ron. *The Cove*, New York: Ecco Press, 2012.

Sloan, Dave U. *Fogy Day and Now, or The World Has Changed*. Atlanta, GA: Foote & Davies, 1891.

Wellman, Manly Wade. *Giant in Gray: A Biography of Wade Hampton of South Carolina*. New York: Scribner, 1949.

Collections and Records

Alan Mason Chesney Medical Archives of the Johns Hopkins Medical Institutions, Baltimore, MD.

Wade Hampton Family Papers, Manuscript Division, Library of Congress, Washington, DC.

Jackson County, NC Deed Book 1, p.393, September 24, 1855, Jackson County Courthouse, Sylva, NC.

Library Museum, Military College of South Carolina, The Citadel, Charleston, SC.

North Carolina Civil War Collection, University of North Carolina, Chapel Hill, NC.

Robert Knox Sneden Diary, 1861–1865 (Mss5:1 Sn237:1), Virginia Historical Society, Richmond, VA.

South Carolina Department of Archives and History, Columbia, SC.

South Carolianiana Library, University of South Carolina, Columbia, SC.

Southern Historical Collection, University of North Carolina, Chapel Hill, NC.

Thomas, William H., *The Tuckseegee and Keowee Turnpike, 1848*: personal papers at Cherokee Museum, Cherokee, NC.

Maps, Photography, Presentations, Pioneers

Cashiers Historical Society

Hot Springs North Carolina Tourism Association, Hot Springs, NC.

William McKee, Wade Hampton Golf Club

Nardy, Jane, Presentation on "Wade Hampton III in Cashiers", Cashiers Historical Society Symposium, May, 2006, Cashiers, NC.

John Rivers, The Chattooga Club

Irv Welling, Cashiers Photography, Cashiers, NC.

Authors

S. Robert Lathan, Jr. M.D.
Bob is a retired internist from Atlanta, Georgia and is a graduate of Davidson College and the Johns Hopkins University School of Medicine. He chaired a symposium on Wade Hampton III in 2006 in Cashiers, North Carolina.

Jane Gibson Nardy
Jane Nardy, of Cashiers, North Carolina, is a retired certified professional genealogist and the historian of the Cashiers Historical Society. At the 2006 symposium of Wade Hampton III, she presented a paper titled, *"Wade Hampton III in Cashiers."*

www.ingramcontent.com/pod-product-compliance
Lightning Source LLC
Chambersburg PA
CBHW042015150426
43196CB00003B/53